D1243276

Weather

Published in the United States of America by Cherry Lake Publishing
Ann Arbor, Michigan
www.cherrylakepublishing.com

Reading Adviser: Marla Conn MS, Ed., Literacy specialist, Read-Ability, Inc.
Content Adviser: Brittany Burchard M.Ed., Science Teacher
Book Design: Jennifer Wahi
Illustrator: Jeff Bane

Photo Credits: © wavebreakmedia / Shutterstock.com, 5; © XiXinXing / Shutterstock.com, 7; © Monkey Business
Images / Shutterstock.com, 9; © Alexey Fedorenko / Shutterstock.com, 11; © anekoho / Shutterstock.com, 13;
© Rickus Groenewald / Shutterstock.com, 15; © Aarti Kalyani / Shutterstock.com, 17; © deepspacedave /
Shutterstock.com, 19; © Maksim Zaytsev / Shutterstock.com, 21; © dotshock / Shutterstock.com, 23; Cover, 2,
3, 6, 8, 12, 24, Jeff Bane

Library of Congress Cataloging-in-Publication Data

Names: Bell, Samantha, author.
Title: Weather / by Samantha Bell.
Description: Ann Arbor : Cherry Lake Publishing, 2018. | Series: My world of
    science | Audience: K to grade 3. | Includes index.
Identifiers: LCCN 2017033513| ISBN 9781534107236 (hardcover) | ISBN
    9781534108226 (paperback) | ISBN 9781534109216 (pdf) | ISBN 9781534120204
    (hosted ebook)
Subjects: LCSH: Weather--Juvenile literature. | Meteorology--Juvenile
    literature.
Classification: LCC QC981.3 .B45 2018 | DDC 551.5--dc23
LC record available at https://lccn.loc.gov/2017033513

Printed in the United States of America
Corporate Graphics

About the author: Samantha Bell has written and illustrated over 60 books for children. She lives in South Carolina with her family and pets.

About the illustrator: Jeff Bane and his two business partners own a studio along the American River in Folsom, California, home of the 1849 Gold Rush. When Jeff's not sketching or illustrating for clients, he's either swimming or kayaking in the river to relax.

There are different kinds of weather. The weather is always changing.

Some days are hot and sunny.
Some days are cold and icy.

What do you wear when it is cold?

Weather changes with the **seasons**. It is warmer in spring and summer. It is cooler in fall and winter.

What is your favorite season?

Some days are cloudy. Clouds are made of tiny water **droplets**.

It rains when clouds have too much water. It snows when the air is cold.

Sometimes it storms. **Electricity** builds up in the clouds. It makes a flash of light. The flash is called lightning.

Lightning causes a loud sound when it strikes. The sound is called thunder.

What do you do during a storm?

Some storms are **dangerous**. Hurricanes have strong winds. Tornados are made of air that spins very fast.

Hurricanes and tornados can **damage** many things. They can damage homes. They can damage cars.

Some **scientists** study the weather. They ask questions. They look for answers.

What would you like to study next?

glossary

damage (DAM-ij) to cause harm to a person or property

dangerous (DAYN-jur-uhs) unsafe; likely to cause harm

droplets (DRAHP-lets) very small drops

electricity (ih-lek-TRIS-ih-tee) a form of energy found in nature

scientists (SYE-uhn-tists) people who study nature and the world we live in

seasons (SEE-zuhnz) the four natural parts of the year

index